Call & Response

Call & Response

POEMS

Forrest Hamer

ALICE JAMES BOOKS
FARMINGTON, MAINE

Acknowledgments

I thank the editors of the following publications for printing several of these poems, sometimes in an earlier version:

Beloit Poetry Journal: "The calling";
Berkeley Poetry Review: "Berkeley, late spring," "Line up"; *Cream City Review:* "Pica";
Drumming Between Us: "Resurrection," "In the blood of you"; *Equinox:* "Touched";
Kenyon Review: "Goldsboro narrative #24: Second benediction";
Olympia Review: "Without John"; *Rain City Review:* "Goldsboro narrative #37";
SFSU Review: "Because we need good maps"; *ZYZZYVA:* "Getting happy"

"Getting happy" also appears in *Best American Poetry 1994,*
ed. A. R. Ammons and D. Lehman (New York: Scribner's, 1994), and in *Strange Attraction,* ed. H. Junker (University of Nevada, 1995).
"Lessons" appears in *Poet's Choice: Poems for Everyday Life,* ed. R. Hass (Ecco, 1998).
"Line up" appears in *Outsiders: Poems about Rebels, Exiles, and Renegades,*
ed. L. Bosselaar (Milkweed, 1999).
"Berkeley, late spring" appears in *The Geography of Home: California's Poetry of Place,*
ed. C. Buckley and G. Young (Heyday, 1999).

Cover photo © 1989 Ken Light from *Delta Time*/Smithsonian Institution Press
Cover and text design: Charles Casey Martin

Alice James Books gratefully acknowledges support from the University of Maine at Farmington, the National Endowment for the Arts, and the Massachusetts Cultural Council, a state agency whose funds are recommended by the Governor, and appropriated by the State Legislature.

Alice James Books are published by
The Alice James Poetry Cooperative, Inc.
University of Maine at Farmington
98 Main Street
Farmington, Maine 04938

To—
Willie Barnes, Sr. (b. 1892)
Emma Haywood Barnes (b. 1890)

Contents

⚔ Wait ⚔

⚔ River ⚔

⚔ Descendant ⚔

⚅ Descent ⚅

Wait

My luck

I could be another body. It could be 1995 or 1959,
or I could live in a time not all that specific.

Lying on the grass last Sunday, or maybe when
I was five, I felt the ground pulling at me.

Apparently, the body has some responsibility.
It plants itself as memory whose accuracy is doubtful:

I could be another. It could be tomorrow.
The earth was pulling, and my body laid out straight

remembered falling asleep in the afternoon, drunk
with play and questions, a find of the four-leaf.

I was lucky all over again: born when I was, to whom,
and where: I was having a good life, a birthday, the day

answering to me. No one I loved had died yet—not
my grandmother who went first and quick, not my brother, not

the others. The breathing of the ground roused me, grass
flooding the nostrils and marking for itself my face.

I woke up belonging somewhere, not yet able to move
for fear I would disturb what was still sleeping.

Getting happy

When the men got happy in church,
   they shouted and jumped straight up.

But the women's trances
   made them dance with moaning; so,

I dreaded Rev. Johnson's sermons
   near their end, hated the trouble

he was causing inside
   the souls of women sweating

and beginning to breathe fast.
   One day, I worried, my mother

would let go and lose herself
   to him, become as giddy

as when my father was coming home
   on leave. Just as silly.

Yet, when it finally happened,
   I felt only left behind.

Years later, another first time,
   I heard my moan echo inside

a girl's ear and recognized
   how woeful pleasure feels.

I then began to wonder
   if there weren't some joy still

to give in to, make me shout
   not as men do but as a woman.

It troubles me.
    I do not have a woman's body

but fear that moaning will betray
    this want in me, or another

to be like a woman. Mostly,
    I fear that moaning will uncover

the love for my mother that is still
    so deep that I want little more

than to be with her as closely as I can.

Uncle

My grandfather's brother was a gravedigger.

He was more than this, I am sure,

but he became little more than parable

to my mother who did not know him well,

who feared him. She says of him

that he was a soldier in the War,

and that he returned to Goldsboro different—

he kept to himself, paced the dirt streets at dusk,

and he begged for work in the graveyards.

After only three days of sculpting out graves,

his dusktime pacing became more agitated,

and he began then to talk back to the dead

still living alongside him. He shouted,

cursed at them, pleaded that they leave him alone

and that they return.

Below and beside

My friends were talking about how a vertical view
of divinity presumes God is above us and male,
the way in families fathers may be head.
They wondered about a lateral sense of things,
God among us on earth, between and therefore within us.

I was listening and I wasn't, thinking at once
about the place of the unconscious to the conscious
—below, presumably, but possibly beside:
a shape in the dark is both a toy chest and a coffin,
someone else a friend as well as a parent

as well as self. I have known for some time
how much there is I do not want to see—
pockets of air where matters wait for me
to notice. Once, while I was visiting back East,
a white woman hanged herself from the invisible.

No one else paid attention, so I saw her
and I didn't. It was the last night's dream,
dreams staying themselves beside what else there is.
Something the matter in my life was beginning to place
itself, the woman not the stranger I could claim.

Probably, my friends were just revisioning
the claim to gods: that God hangs alongside
awful between us, no longer dominating.

Erection

I wanted them bad: the mail-order x-ray glasses
that looked straight through clothes to bodies—

of those in my class, of the old-lady teacher
who wore miniskirts and an opened blouse, of grownups

whose eyes stopped meeting mine. I wanted to see
a privacy clothes know: the geography of the possible.

I waited.

And when the glasses hadn't come, and each day's
disappointment stung like slaps,

I worried that other people could see hard-ons hidden
by long-tailed shirts worn outside the pants,

by a walk-become-a-race, or by the distraction
of stubborness and anger. And arrogance.

Wondered if they could see how timid the penis
otherwise seemed, how fat still my chest was,

making improbable breasts. Wondered if they could
see the tenseness of no-more-but-not-yet,

of sleep-erupting dreams having nothing to do with the body
and everything, desire becoming specific.

And when the glasses still hadn't come
and there was cause to doubt their existence,

I began to imagine what I might see,
bodies nothing like those I have seen.

The calling

◪ Text: A slave ship sinks in the Atlantic, 1749.

There must have been a great noise: the drumming and slap
of limbs against wood, ankles fit slack in shackles.

Children, there must have been a trembling violence,
bodies once more roused from a lumber of days, drunk
from the odor of shit and stilled in middle dance.

And, yes, there were terrible voices, the holler
wresting itself out, shouts silencing what babies
would tell, silencing even the goodness of God.

Don't you know there was a joy? that revenge came down
upon the men who chained them, who chained and locked them,
who would not look at them closely, not in the eyes;
that revenge had come from the body's dark water
to claim them all, even those who rendered feeling,
who swallowed and swallowed, swallowed deeply, then died.

And there must have been a moaning song that the land
heard about the deep grief of ocean, coward sky,
the brashness of resisting winds. Quiet
moves us to the edge of land and we lay ourselves
on it to listen; or, we lay ourselves inside.

Aside from spirits, I was alone there,
and after I had cut the grass, put the mower back in the car,
    I lingered at my grandparents' graves.

The sun settled while the air cooled itself off,
and dark trailed the oldest parts of the cemetery
    in full skirts. As I heard her slowly approach,

I imagined a hand come through the ground
as if the ground were as weightless as water,
and the hand calmly closed itself at my ankle,

my Mama Emma asking, *Stay, son*
    even though I could leave if I would
my Papa Willie said, *Yes. Stay, son*

                    I was soon going North
to college, I told them; I was excited. I talked
about Mom becoming saved, Dad retiring from the Army,

my sister and the boy she secretly loved, my brother and how mean
    we were to each other without meaning to be,
        my dead brother whose grave no one had visited much.

And I told them what I had not been wanting to tell them—
that I had not been called to preach.
    I admitted I was feeling relieved, no longer worried

    about ignoring an unmistakable voice,
daring then to live in defiance of a terrible holy command
    to surrender and surrender again.

The dark stopped and nothing else moved,
    not even the waters of the ear, not even the heart.
    And when my grandparents finally spoke,

    they spoke with voices I have not yet recognized,
    reminded me to pray and to be good
    to people and to come back and sit with them at dusk.

The dark moved on again, and clouds watched
me leave, the whole night smelling
suddenly of the saltwater roaring in my nose.

Ⱥ

A story my grandfather used to love
to tell had to do with his own baptism.
The preacher walked him into the muddy Neuse River
and they stood in there for a moment,
both of them dressed in white, both of them light.
And as my grandfather, a boy, really,
folded his arms across his chest—the way
dead people sometimes do—the church members sang
Just As I Am. When the preacher embraced him,
and my grandfather began to fall
easily into deepness, a snake swam near enough
for them both to see. My grandfather threw
himself out of the preacher's arms, ran to land;
and the chuckling preacher called him back, for
he had seen many snakes in that river
and this serpent was not one to fear.

In my swimming class, I am chuckling at my fear
of snakes in the pool. I hate the term Dead Man's Float,
but trust the teacher when he says I will
later feel calm and forget what I am
doing. What I am doing is what I have tried
to learn twice before—how to breathe underwater,
how to trust that water entering my one good ear
will leave again, how to let water embrace
my body into descent. At the moment,
it is hardest to let my hips dance in that deep
space; the teacher has told us that men's trunks sink
our legs below the surface of water,
and this seems easily like sex. Yet,
the serpent waiting low in that water
is probably unconcerned with sin.
What is really making me feel naked in this class
is the presence of another black man.

...and they saw not their father's nakedness.
—Genesis 9:23

They walk in backwards.
They cover Noah.

Ham tries to forget what he has seen.
He tries to forget

that his father has only a man's body
His father is no God

Ham tries to forget the bending, the scars, the whiting hair

Ham tries to forget the penis, its tender shape

He tries to forget the shoulders gone round, the dragging chest

To forget breath, the craven let breath

And Ham tries to forget a prophecy
of his own short life which is now shorter than before
because his own body sometimes bends,

voices beckoning

River

Night traveling

...*long before HIV, there was a sense both men and women
had of being rushed by sex into oblivion....*
—Linsey Abrams

Because we are unsatisfied, and because we can,
we look into someone's eyes
that might love us and we ask, Come—
Take me from this

We want to cease. No, we want the body
to cease. And, because it also wants this,
we look for some other
shape we might become then,
upon return.

Take me, you said.

The next morning, early, I remembered
the dream: the long flight keeling
away on the back of a black bird,
how sights cleared just at perception;
that someone laughed, whoever I was, scared at
the chill beneath desire, under all sky.

Berkeley, late spring

I'd been browsing the poetry section at Cody's

and as I walked out, the unexpected sun lighted the lips
of everyone in the Friday afternoon crowd along Telegraph,
and I imagined kissing them all: nestling mine
with pouted lips, wrinkling lips, some faded and practical,
others comfortably possessed. Thought how funny
folks would think me if they knew, then how rare
in all our lives these reverences are (like being next
to another as they sleep, or rest); imagined what their smells
were, the sun now steaming the air around us:
and if the smells would matter, sweet or rank; decided
then to write of it, save in the spaces between words
elusive want.

and remembered kissing my first girlfriend inside a church
before aching out goodbye; remembered kissing my grandmother
three days dead and laid out for respects all night
before the funeral, her face cool and newly taut, the kiss
protecting me from fearing her spirit come back to sleep
        beside me;
remembered how a lover kissed, his tongue tracing desire
        along rivers
of my body (and now that he is dead, too, the traces make me
        anxious: as if
a spirit—his, or another's—walks with me along this street
and everywhere); remembered how at moments even now
        watching strangers kiss
goodbye leaves my lips just enough warm.

and I noticed that the poems that moved me
had mostly to do with loving and loss and the loss of love
and I wondered when it would be time to be moved by
        other poems
not haunted by fears of wanting and remembering.
And I've noticed that this poem is not the one

I thought it'd be because the smells that move along rivers
in our breathing have mattered after all; because spaces
between all these words hold there more complicated wishes
than for casual prayers within a motley crowd.

Goldsboro narrative #14:
Faith healing

At Berniece Lane's homegoing service,
the preacher insisted we clap, not feel sad,

know Berniece had shed her young life to be free—

of the spreading cancer, the husband who flaunted
a girlfriend, the thick work of picking tobacco.

The preacher railed against a plain misery
of women in makeup and in body-shaping clothes:

misery of a woman's desire for the man
she has married but sometimes has not met. And

those of us not from this denomination
wondered why God decided not to save
Berniece Lane, did not treat this wife better.

For, was the preacher therefore jealous

that this woman would meet God before she would,
the miseries finally slipped from her body

like a shirt with no room for breasts?

Goldsboro narrative #36

Before Friday dusk, after the factory had let out,
Miss Gert had gone round to all the places they sold liquor—

the Meeks', whose still was hid by pecan trees;
Yelverton's kitchen near the railroad tracks; and,
if you had got paid that day, the ABC store downtown.

When my sister and I had finished our homework
and my grandparents were fixing to fall asleep,

my mother took us home, and we would always stir Miss Gert
with our car's disapproving headlights. Hey!
she'd shout before her body cleared itself in the dust,

and when we'd hey her back I noticed in her reddened eyes
the reverence of church mothers anointing Holy Children

during Sunday morning prayer. By Sunday night service, though,
Miss Gert looked like the long weekend she'd had,
and she sometimes stood outside in that other dusk calling

in, not to the mothers, but to the children
beginning to thirst for some first taste.

Pica

an abnormal desire for unusual foods

I'd noticed the flowers first, wondered if
the orange I saw in the pink of them was
actual or an idea of mine,
something descriptive which had become real.

I still don't know, but in his office
that morning we talked about how soil tastes.

The dirt nearest my grandmother's hollyhocks was
the best. Shades of black smelled of stories
I hadn't yet heard that would linger
in my nose through night—these would be places

to grow things, grow: lay inside some seed then each day
resurrect the forming curl and green of them.

Stories change things, even the dead things laid there.
So when my grandmother was buried,
and there could be no digging and redigging,
I imagined the darkness was changing her

night by night: her face sank while hairs raised themselves
like fur, her nails grew long and rounded, and

each dim wrinkle dried into another.
By the eightieth night, I noticed
that her skin had worn itself away, and how
her pink dress loosely framed her shape of bones.

And there were stories in the soil
about where she'd gone and the people I knew

only by name that she'd seen again. She
was learning other stories to tell me,
and she whispered them in my deepening sleep.
I had forgot the story about the night

the soil erased her and she was anything
but brightness in grains. But I was

sitting in his office one morning
complaining of no dreams, and the idea
of orange made those flowers smell dank,
and I became alive, craving.

His assumption

Our encyclopedia had each volume but its S,
for I would stash that fat book in the attic
or under the house, banishing those 19 pages, banishing snakes
from casual access, having slayed
this time I hoped for good the blood red dragon
whose wings I had taken for myself, folding them flat
behind me, wondering how a boy wears wings
not originally his own, particularly when
he has murdered something and is no longer
afraid of it.
                No one loved Him as much
as Lucifer, I was told. But even the love of angels
is not perfect and is easily betrayed.

The fall from him was endless

Ordinary fidelity

Before the baby is loved, it can be hated
and the mother who loves the older child considers
this, and is indifferent—she tends,
knows love will probably come. And, probably,
her son will love it too, but, before,
he will devise what he can to kill it.

                    The baby dies.
Oh! It wasn't supposed to, something in the wanted
not yet clear, not final. It was supposed to go
away, not there, the place it went, but to another
place: nothing to do with memory or grief:
nothing to do with a responsibility each new love is
for the rest of his life.

               His mother goes on loving him, and
she loves him without having to love
other children.

           She does not hate him at all.

Lesson

It was 1963 or 4, summer,
and my father was driving our family
from Ft. Hood to North Carolina in our 56 Buick.
We'd been hearing about Klan attacks, and we knew

Mississippi to be more dangerous than usual.
Dark lay hanging from trees the way moss did,
and when it moaned light against the windows
that night, my father pulled off the road to sleep.

Noises
that usually woke me from rest afraid of monsters
kept my father awake that night, too,
and I lay in the quiet noticing him listen, learning
that he might not be able always to protect us

from everything and the creatures besides;
perhaps not even from the fury suddenly loud
through my body about this trip from Texas
to settle us home before he would go away

to a place no place in the world
he named Viet Nam. A boy needs a father
with him, I kept thinking, fixed against noise
from the dark.

Down by the riverside

Ain't goin study war no more
Ain't goin study war no more
Ain't goin study war no more

During the time Daddy was becoming Dad,
the armies and armies of green plastic soldiers
went on with their wars, my empire of the private
grown. Walter Cronkite tallied each day's casualties,
and my soldiers named themselves Americans or Viet Cong;
they zipped themselves up in long full bags or lay about
without their arms and legs. My soldiers bloodied themselves
with our garden's mud, and they did so under orders
from the eight-year-old sergeant whose father
had not been home in months.

And since I had not seen him,
even in the crowds laughing at Bob Hope jokes,
a new crowd each new place, I commanded
that the Army needed chaplains more than sergeants,
and the next Sunday I joined church, begged God
to help me lay down burdens and bring Dad home;
and that day I baptized each of my soldiers
in large garden puddles, blessed the crowd of them at
attention, and studied them not once more.

Because we need good maps

At this age of his when he wasn't here,

I study my imagination for the father
of the nine-year-old me, the adventures

exciting him way off across a globe

with no country on it named Viet Nam.
I have to go find him, the man who came back

a stranger. My father must still be roaming,

charting lost locations for this year of mine
which marks the journey I can't start.

Without John

His things: clothes smelling still of him
(four suits—two of them grey, seven pants,
12 shirts, his bathrobe, nine pairs of shoes
and one of heavy boots, far too many ties,
four wool sweaters and a full wool coat,
many sorts of red briefs, socks and socks),
letters and copies of some he sent, pictures
left loose in batches, his journal, his will,
five dozen albums, books and books about books,
cancelled checks, his glasses, his razor,
his watch, his special pens, his sweats,
colognes and creams, keys, his basketball,
his sleeping bag and tent, his toothbrush,
more keys.

Last respects

Although I have never seen him naked, I think
my uncle should be buried without clothes.

And I will tell my aunt this when she asks
which suit of his we should dress him in, and

whether I will shave him one last time.
As if it matters.

                        As if we should not show
the slow stripping of the body toward its own

revelation. The way a single lifetime accustoms
and resists what we keep asking it to tell us.

Let us bury him naked. Let us leave him unshaven.
Leave him alone this time.

Sculpture

The length of my arm, stretched full, the half height
of my long body;

a hand, spread;
my finger or the thought of my finger;

the shadow beyond an edge that marks what I am and what
you are or life is or I am not of—

I have been keeping these distances.

What there is within distance is what
I have shaped in a space between
the outside and the inside I look into the outside from.

There, an uncle came to see
spirits fleshed human: his attention became claimed
by them: he did not live again in the world.

The world is not the distance I have wanted
to talk about. I want to talk about my father.

My father withdraws when his body hurts.
My father suffers and then he withdraws.

My uncle appears right here
at the edge between my father and me, acknowledges
the companion he sees in my body

bending itself into my father's hurt, holding it
away by the arm or the thought of an arm.

Arboretum

As for purpose with a capital P,

I suppose this is what Bronk refers to when he writes

life isn't about us; it's about itself....

I walk gardens with benches placed in groves

of the quiet: I accept what he says. Yet, I don't

understand this grieving we do, the holding

on. Maybe Purpose is also inherent to grief,

the names benchplates announce as evidence:

love survives only as long as it needs to.

Resurrection

You think you might die. You think you've stopped breathing

and you might die; yet, your eyes don't leave his face,
you let him kiss the stretch of your neck,
you smell each other. This you do

until you give breath back
which no longer belongs to the same life,

which is a blessing.

Descendant

Surrendered

I was thinking about the illusion
of objectivity, and of course
I thought of you and what you think. No—
I wonder if you think about the last time we
talked, the disruption you expected
me to explain. Well, I had wanted you
completely, but found the want impossible
because you were not willing
to be stolen away to me. Something
dense scattered itself across the space
like clouds, and the apathy I felt thickened
breathing. I had to make myself
find meaning, and when again I had,
I talked myself into talking to you.

The anthropologist I'd been eager to meet
said he believes black Americans
are paranoid for believing
in a genocide conspiracy. The matter is
a strangle. Histories of peoples reduce then
to an argument between clinical ideas.
And, no longer listening, I long
for something true I might surrender to.

Once, during sex, I felt sensation dull
and noticed the absurdness to that play,
compulsions all the same. I wonder if this is
the danger between us or if you'd argue
that desire is all desire is, lasting
past the hiding and disguise when two of us
are talking through ideas.

Text:

After a friend died, he had a tear just fallen tattooed
from the left of his left eye

> *The poems have not been written*
> *Bravely*

and each time after
another tear fell, until there was no more space

> *And so they have spoken of niggers*
> *Not imagining even the nigger was listening.*

then drops cascaded down across his neck over
his shoulders
down

> *Words creating world*
> *Own no independent meaning;*

the length of his slight body.
This was attractive to people. They wondered what it felt like

> *Those of us learning language*
> *Decipher using context.*

to be entered by him, this grave man not apparently afraid
of anything:

Goldsboro narrative #11

I sorely do love her, I thought he said.
Actually, he said he loved her surely,
but Southerners mix words up sometimes
and I have often taken them at face value.

So, as this Southern man was talking about
the Southern woman he would marry,

it seemed to me grownups tangled their feelings
unnecessarily, and especially love. And,
since we were in Goldsboro and it was 1969,
I thought the confusion had to do with race—

with whether integration would work, even
if we called it desegregation (he didn't

believe it would.) Or maybe she didn't love him at all
but was afraid to die by herself and
he was as good as the men who wouldn't come along:
surely this could work. That word again.

On the face of it, we know things and we know
even that we don't. We don't seem to do well with

the rest—whatever it is that trips
chaos into *talk-and-listen,* makes us mix up things.
Or, if race doesn't really explain, then
how do we explain these feelings we have about race?

I was asking the man how he thought our town would do
sending different children to the same schools.

He was in love, he protested, and he just wanted
the South to stay as it was for now,
not get into tangling things.

Allegiance

I loved the Supremes as much as baseball
at eleven, my first base plate a stage.
So in those summertime lulls in action,
all base hits easily thwarted, I sang
the way Diana Ross did—rare and
heavy-lidded, often about some love
that did her wrong. The background girls concurred.
And I noticed myself changing pronouns,
suddenly aware that the other boys
listened closely to their first baseman,
more now than he had, reminding him
how necessary practice is with pronouns,
converting he to she at every turn;
otherwise a guy on the other team
might get past you, and then another one
could bat him in, the other side winning
and your whole team holding you responsible.

Goldsboro narrative #17

When the town's Negro children went to the white school
to hear the North Carolina Symphony, we crossed lines

between music from our churches, radio and records
and music of violins and muted brass.

                                    The first time
I heard "The Firebird", I felt the sudden threat of tears

that sometimes held me tremble in a preacher's voice
or in a harmony of saxophones.

                    Within them all, theme was offered; then,
fine elaboration: how much there is to know

about a soul kept sealed inside a place not made
for enchantment.

                            And then there is your life—

not at all immortal or protected by the magic of a feather;
instead, it seizes arbitrary meaning in lines drawn wide

and improvises foolishly.

The fit of old customs

᛭

It becomes the story
about how ways change over time according
        to an urgency the young feel to insist themselves
                in history, insist history
        is new; about

        how children of slaves felt
a freedom their freed parents did not share,
                and each set of children kept freedom
        as if there was only enough for them;

about the *and-so-on* of this which is
        the march I notice within myself, approaching
        forty, startled that
        a generation younger than mine refers warmly
                to each other as niggers, the word between them
not merely the shackle it could always be for me.

"*My father was born and brought up as a slave.
He never knew anything else until after I
was born. He was taught his place and was
content to keep it. But when he brought
me up he let some of the old customs slip by.
But I know there are certain things that I
must do and I do them, and it doesn't worry me;
yet, in bringing up my own son I let some more
of the old customs slip by. For a year I have
been keeping him from going to Chicago; but he
tells me this is his last crop; that in the fall
he's going. He says 'When a young white man
talks rough to me, I can't talk rough to him.
You can stand that; I can't. I have some
education, and inside I has the feelings of a
white man. I'm going.*"

Even when you know your place, you know
a place isn't yours. And if you stay there,

if you drape yourself in cloth that was not made
for you, that strains at the middle and the neck
or cannot hang from hips or from the shoulders,

then you let your children go naked
until they begin wanting to leave you,

and you cover them with stories about nakedness
and the ways a cloth can feel, and you tell them
stories about your father and his place

so when they one day read a story about an emperor
duped by his weavers to parade arrogance,

your children recognize themselves
at least in the boy who tells what he sees,
at most in the father who listens.

Goldsboro narrative #37

The two men, the father and the son, won't reconcile,
even when the father is dying
                        and the son has been called,
because the woman each has loved the most has left them,
                        and each man blames the other.
And one will have a dream
that the other has been murdered, will wake up chilly
and think of a winding road near railroad tracks.
It should be walked
            —he tells himself—
                        one of us should walk it,
but as a train rails past,
a woman on it wonders
                who he is and so he wonders what to answer.
The son in them will want only for daughters
and the father that God is not after all male.
                        And, grasses will grow over the dirt
of the road each man will dream about for years, and when
the woman wants to come back,
                        she will have no way of finding them.

Touched

Sometimes, when there are tears in my eyes,
I conclude I must be mourning again.
This is wrong, I'm beginning to think, for sadness
seems too simple a conclusion to what brings on this quiet.
It may have something to do with awe.

The quiet has something to do with awe.
I repeat this, hoping the rhythm will give me
words. I hear, instead, myself humming
to an angry boy who would not speak to me but
would not let me leave his glare. We held on to each other
    like this.

The angry boy held on to me while I hummed.
I was his counselor and we were touching
what is raw and aching somewhere in us all
but concentrated in his life and in that hour
when his hatred loosed what I then heard so I could hold him
    back.

My humming to him helped me hold him back—
not in the sense of restraining but of responding.
It seems to matter here what the meanings are of holding,
and if touching is the same as being touched
the way in craziness we throw our tearful selves against
    the quiet.

Tearfulness has something to do with being touched.
Maybe I had held him back the way I hadn't meant
just then: my fears of being touched in anything
but loud familiar ways reminds me now there is more violence
than mourning ever saves us from, more hatred than two might
    ever hold.

My fear of hatred made me hold him back.
Sometimes the violence I learn about in quiet

silences the hums I think distract me
from feeling humble. That boy from years ago
has killed himself; since then we sit together quietly
    for hours at a time.

The boy now dead sits quietly with me.
I'm moved by something awful I can't name:
it is a grace. I'm learning more
about the complicated laying on of hands that heals
through a mercy of the fearless.

Goldsboro narrative #23:
First day of desegregation, 1969

The two girls fixing

to fight each other
the first day of eighth grade

were wildly close.

And those of us watching
could smell them

and the possibility
that one might leap

into the privacy

all of us were keeping
from strangers.

Line up

Once again, someone took me
for another black man, my brother
and someone else's, who robbed a store
or took a woman's precious,
stole back something lost to him. Someone
came up to me, slapped me in my face,
and made me prove I was not criminal
or minded of crime: told me
open up my coat and produce
that bottle of gin,
                    that driver's license,
                                        that penis
they swore they saw me put there
as I'd gone about my business
                    presuming it belonged to me.

A boy doesn't know

A boy does not know these things.
He plays with himself, engages
others,
     but he doesn't understand
why lying on his stomach
         or on his back with raised legs
and having the man edge himself past
          and then inside
is what the man really wants him to do.
A boy doesn't know

      and so he leaves himself
lying on a bed or on a floor or up against a wall;
he watches and he waits,
pulls up his pants and wonders what to do
   with the stickiness on his fingers, how to take himself
     from that place to another.

After the semen dries and the clothes from that day
have been buried, he spends forever
trying to remember if the numbness that flared
in his nostrils and consumed all air
distracted him from noticing the yank and tug
there *must* have been when something in his middle
not yet named, yet missed,
was taken easily as breath.

Taking care

Behind me, a man began playing harmonica.
It was annoying. I was trying to read.

When he finished, he murmured something
and walked the aisle back to front holding out

his knitted cap. Two trips, and the cap
was empty, not even a dime.

He stared dull at a baby boy two rows
ahead of me who had continued to dance,

who giggled loud each time he threw himself back
against his father as if to fall,

the father catching him every time.

Goldsboro narrative #5:
Elders the grandchildren of slaves

Long before the burning cross could flame
away into ashes, the elders arranged
to have the fire on the neighbor's lawn

doused, and by morning there was no
evidence for children that the
neighborhood had been visited. Sent

to my room to play, I overheard the worry
that had been snuffed a minute before,
and I looked out my window for even

a shadow on the Negro leader's yard.
When my grandfather told me that afternoon
how good I was, how much as good as anyone

else, I knew he was preparing my sister and me
for the day we would walk into a classroom
full of white children and find a seat.

It wasn't the news of the cross burning
that elders protected us from, not the news
of a bombed church somewhere else,

of Sunday-after-church lynchings, or
the real reason we would drink water
at home before going downtown, but

the bitterness and the worry and the fear,
quickenings that flare terrible,
recalling what their grandparents learned.

A child couldn't walk into that classroom
knowing what the elders knew. A child
wouldn't look for a seat in that room

if he knew what the elders knew. A child
wouldn't play outside even into dark
if the child really believed

visitors would come into his neighborhood
wearing white sheets so they could light up a night
elders might not be able to calm.

Appointment

we talk on for hours
pretending to ourselves
we understand these conversations. But
minutes after drifting into bed away from you
that old dead slave visits, keeps me
awake with disturbing speeches
And, droned into sleep, my dreams are crazy
and I sweat all over

into day
At work my duties are distracting.
Later hours wait — my breath quickens
and becomes loud — I meet you —
And we continue

talking for hours   meanings misunderstood
And, minutes after, I am sure: he returns,
sits on my bed, lowers the light
and begins

Descent

Slave song

for Sterling Brown

Don't want to be singin no slave songs.
Slavery is over, and I don't want to hear em.
I don't care about rememberin old things.
Don't be bringin no slave songs.

Slavery is over, and I don't want to hear em.
My feets can move just as free as they please.
Don't be bringin no slave songs.
Don't be askin bout no slave shuffle.

My feets can move just as free as they please.
I got no need to stay in one place.
Don't be askin bout no slave shuffle.
A body cain't barely feel itself that way.

I got no need to stay in one place.
Don't go speakin to me bout no religion.
A body cain't barely feel itself that way.
God ain't done nothin but look at me and grin.

Don't go speakin to me bout no religion.
My old master think hisself God's onliest son.
God ain't done nothin but look at me and grin.
Freedom ain't come from none of these ways.

My old master think hisself God's onliest son.
I don't care about rememberin old things.
Freedom ain't come from none of these ways.
Don't want to be singin no slave songs.

Choir practice

...make a joyful noise
—Psalms 81:1

A

At the moment my grandfather whoa'd his mule,
looked up away from the sun, dried his face,

I noticed him imagining, and I called

to him there from Yale one whole boyhood later,

writing a paper about the songs he'd been
singing, wishing him finally to visit.

I was having trouble thinking, had gone impatient

with the stink of humid manure. Too slowly,
earth gave up its platted roots so something new could sink

and grow and, later, grow again.

"What'd you say to Old Red, Papa Willie? What'd you say?",

my grandfather grinning, his daughter's boy reading
under a tree until it was time to go on
home for middle-day supper.

I called to him again.

A slave woman ranting, rocking herself
most nights near my bed, waited for me
to turn over, look
at the scars boning her back, look
at her again, grief thick in the red folds of her eye.
She waited to talk to me.
She had lost her son and she waited to talk to me.

Beginning her visits then, when
I said I would not write again, would not sing
anymore in the gospel choir. I said
I had too many classes, needed more work-study time,
wanted back my Wednesday nights.
And there was nothing else to write about.

Her son had been sold away, and she wailed
for him, went inside herself, went away.
She had gone far into vigil, waiting
restless in night, calling
into ears of men who might know of him,
who might be calling to her with news.

I am not the one, I told her. I do not know him.
But you have called him, she said. No—
I called my grandfather, listened for his voice
in the middle of my long walks, listened
when I turned my left ear up against night,
the other tuned into the tremble in my dreaming.
My grandfather is not your son.

Honey, honey, honey, look what you done,
You done made me love you, and now your woman done come.
If anybody ask you who wrote this lonesome song,
Tell 'em you don't know the writer,
but a lonesome woman put it on.
　　—Ma Rainey song written by T. A. Dorsey

She
tilted back her head
and let
　　　　　　breath,
some note we had forgot
possible in this life—

She tilted
back her head, occasioning music, sounding
the body, abandoning us—

She
tilted back her head, taking
our hands, Abraham before God at that altar,
willing to kill—

She tilted
back her head, trebling
ancient objections,
home dispersing and dispersed, dispersing—

She
tilted back her head and let what we had lost return
to bless us.

✻

The elders arrived early with lumbering sways,
the day heavy in them, the hard half-week bowing
them toward Wednesday evening's choir practice.

Maybe a blessing would come. Maybe the Holy Spirit
would visit them there, the church lights mute
with a common night's discomfort. Maybe a blessing.

The others came, asking after each other.
How's your mama. Your daddy. Mr. Him. Miss Her.
Respects beckoned clear as calls,

                              so when the choir director came
later but not late, he answered their voices with piano
                              and someone offered up prayers.

They rehearsed first the old hymns, notes distinct,
songs asking after each business
of tithes, morning Scripture, the announcements.

And then spirituals, multiple dance and claps
calling across for visitation, for inspiration,
voices improvising each other.

They practiced marching in, starting at temple's end,
step-and-step-to, swaying all listeners
                              Rise.

And, late, younger children asleep on the pews,
older ones humming and fancying how we would one day leave
our parents, not yet knowing if we would

want to come back, the elders prayed another prayer,
the half-week before Sunday standing among us,
now respectful, lighter, almost making promises.

Look at me again, she asked, abrupt in the chair.
What does your grandfather think of you,
white people speaking through your voice,
their history yours? Has he come to you here?
How would he know to find you? Why
have you come here if not to sing?

There is nothing I can write about, I said.
I do not have words, no language
for what has happened to me in this place
I have wanted to belong to, which shames me
and asks me over and over to prove
I am not ashamed of myself. I make no home here.

You are a black man. Yes, I am
an American black man who cannot write
about anything, who is waked by screaming
old slaves looking in him for lost children,
looking in his memory for songs.
As if I have heard them—

Tell me, if you find them in me, will you rest?
Will you hear yourself singing with them, and rest?
And if your daughters and your sons are
also white, also Indian, and you hear yourself
singing in them, will you rest?

He won't visit you if you don't sing.
Your grandfather will not come here if you don't
listen close to yourself
singing, the way you laid yourself against
his chest, listening to him laugh,
breathing his stories, listening to him

as he sang, his voice old
and clear, particular; listened for songs
of people you do not know who loved you as
their own; heard the history of
your body, its languages,
the lives in them you could be speaking.

*Thomas A. Dorsey wrote the song "Take my hand, precious Lord"
in 1932, just after his wife and newborn son had died.*

He must have hated the Lord.

Must have hated the Lord who loved him
so much he would take away his only child
and wife to have him, this Lord
who loved him too much to let him love.

Must have hated the Lord who forsaked
him, disbelief stunning the will, will stunned
by this betrayal.

Hatred must have rushed full against his ears like noise,
loud sound leaving him deaf.
So much he could not speak.

He must have dropped, felled
from some arrogance he did not imagine
could disturb Him.

Must have drowned himself in memory of her—
ache she had for the new one, one within,
giving her first dreams of calm
water, given, listening. Children:

He must have hated the Lord so much he could not stand
but love Him.

Lord, the moaning

Instead of radio gospel music, my father played
an Eddie Harris record that Sunday morning.
Exodus to Jazz, I think.

My mother disapproved.
Cousin Fannie had come by the Friday night before
to remind her she had been raised better than this—

not taking her children to Sunday School and church.
She said my dead grandmother had visited
to find out about the baby

she did not know had died.
And my grandmother asked this cousin to come by
and console, return her daughter's family to the fold.

My father insisted we should go on without him.
He would stay at home, worship God some other way
none of us would hear.

And when he was alone,
he played piano as he had before his mother died—
he and his brothers moving congregations in quartet.

He thought of my mother who had stopped dancing Coltrane,
who stilled herself mourning for their son. He listened
to the apparitions

that would finally bring her back.

In the blood of you, hearing gives itself and takes

Ancient things remain in the ears.
—Ashanti proverb

*How does a tribe
come to be?*

The first time a lover loved my ears,

*How,
in those moments
a soul is borne,*

tongued and chewed and nibbled them,

*does blood become
itself—a river*

I felt a roar and heard

*waving
wanderers
to cross it*

blood rush itself to answer

and be home

Goldsboro narrative #24:
Second benediction

Knowing we still needed to dance,
the man who kept company with men

played the church organ sassy

and let us sway ourselves near him
even as we gathered still beside him,

watching his thin fingers talk the way they dared

when the sermon had been made
and we lingered to pray for sound

because the body waits for sound. We waited

for the moment his fingers spoke in their tongues,
listened for the urgent translation into this:

We have returned to a blessed place;
Our family is here with us, even the dead and not-born;
We are journeying to the source of all wonder,

We journey by dance. Amen.

for Mr. Holman

Notes

Call-and-response is an African music pattern wherein the relationship between leader and chorus is described through the interaction of the overlapping voices.

"My luck." This poem was inspired by an essay by Adam Phillips, "Contingency for Beginners" (in *On Flirtation*, Harvard, 1994) wherein he writes, "one can often reconstruct very interesting bits of people's histories from their accounts of their luck."

"Night traveling." The epigraph is taken from an essay by Linsey Abrams, "Gay pride," printed in Colorado Review, Fall 1994.

"Arboretum." The phrase appears in William Bronk's poem "The life" published in *Manifest; and Furthermore*, North Point Press, 1987.

"The fit of old customs." The second section is a quote cited in *Negro migration in 1916-1917*, U. S. Department of Labor, Division of Labor; George Haynes, editor, 1919, p. 33.

"Choir practice." The composer Thomas A. Dorsey (1900–1993) is the subject of Michael W. Harris's *The Rise of Gospel Blues: The Music of Thomas Andrew Dorsey in the Urban Church*, Oxford, 1992.

Ⓐ

For their helpful comments on the manuscript, I thank Lynne Knight, Dan Bellm, Molly Fisk, Carol Potter, E. J. Miller Laino, Doug Anderson, Deborah DeNicola, Ted Deppe, and Dorianne Laux. I also thank the writers in the LaVereda Road group, as well as the Bay Area Writer's Workshop. I am particularly grateful for the inspiring teaching of Robert Hass and Yusef Komunyakaa.

Photo: Kwanlam Wong

Forrest Hamer was born in North Carolina in 1956, and was educated at Yale and at Berkeley. He is a psychologist living and working in Oakland, California; a lecturer in psychology at the University of California, Berkeley; and a candidate at the San Francisco Psychoanalytic Institute. This is his first book.

Recent Titles from Alice James Books

Margaret Lloyd, *This Particular Earthly Scene*
Jeffrey Greene, *To the Left of the Worshiper*
Timothy Liu, *Vox Angelica*
Suzanne Matson, *Durable Goods*
Jean Valentine, *The River at Wolf*
David Williams, *Traveling Mercies*
Rita Gabis, *The Wild Field*
Deborah DeNicola, *Where Divinity Begins*
Richard McCann, *Ghost Letters*
Doug Anderson, *The Moon Reflected Fire*
Carol Potter, *Upside Down in the Dark*

Alice James Books has been publishing poetry since 1973. One of
the few presses in the country that is run collectively, the cooperative
selects manuscripts for publication and the new authors become active
members of the press, participating in editorial and production activities.
The press was named for Alice James, sister of William and Henry,
whose gift for writing was ignored and whose fine journal did not
appear until after her death.